She Tells Us Stories:
Experiences and Epiphanies

She Tells Us Stories:
Experiences and Epiphanies

Eleanor Stewart

Jules' Poetry Playhouse Publications
Albuquerque, NM

Eleanor Stewart
Jan. 10, 2018

In memory of
Dr. Edward T. Hall

Professor of Anthropology, author of "The Silent Language"
who told me that I didn't need a degree in cultural anthropology, I just
needed to keep an open mind and observe.

Cover photo: Eleanor Stewart, Kitase Studios, Kamakura, Japan.
Cover design: Denise Weaver Ross

Price: $15.00
ISBN-13: 978-1977888679
ISBN-10: 1977888674
Copyright © 2017 Jules' Poetry Playhouse Publications

Acknowledgements

The College Girl appeared in *Fixed & Free Anthology* (Mercury Heartlink)

My Poor Little Hometown appeared in *Water,* Vol. 3 of the Poets Speak Anthology (Beatlick Press & Jules' Poetry Playhouse Publications)

Snake Dance appeared in *Shadow of the Snake* (Jules' Poetry Playhouse Publications)

On Camino Militar and Quick Sketch appeared in *Falling Into Enchantment* (Sunstone Press)

The Walls of Time forthcoming in *Walls,* Vol. 4 of the Poets Speak Anthology (Beatlick Press & Jules' Poetry Playhouse Publications)

Table of Contents

I – EXPERIENCES

Theater is the World

New Mexico – A New-Old World

Teaching is Learning

Refugee Suite

Wombats and Cobras

My Japan

I – EXPERIENCES

THEATER IS THE WORLD

From 15 to 32, acting was my real world
Rehearsing or performing in the evenings
After that, I didn't know where to go at night

The College Girl

She walked around the small town of Marietta
As though she were an explorer
Her uniform was black tights and ballet slippers
A brown velveteen tunic like Robin Hood's
Or else a brown wool sweater with two wear holes in it
Now this wasn't the Village in NYC
This was Ohio—home of blending in
She wore her innocent armor to say
"I am in the theatre—in my own imagined world"
She was 18 and had long brown hair
She walked alone but I don't remember lonely
Later there was lots of lonely
But then she was proudly self sufficient
And here's the thing
She was safe—not a thought of danger
Except from the mighty river that flowed nearby
She had been taught to fear its power
But only river rats hung out down there
And she was a Theatre Person
Who wanted to be seen as a tragic heroine
But everyone said she looked happy all the time
Hello and goodbye, young Eleanor
No way you could recognize me now
You didn't dream how far I'd go from that little college town
How far from the theatre
And yet how deep into the drama of the world
I look plenty tragic now, romantic foolish girl
And all it took was sorrow, pain and lots and lots of time

As Lady Capulet, in "Romeo and Juliet"
for Joseph Papp's Shakespeare in the Park, 1970
(photo credit Frank Derbas)

The Actress

She had been warned about New York City
Her fatherly professor said it would break her heart
And he made sure her grad school was for teachers
         and not Carnegie Tech
She had done many roles before she got there
         modern and classical
         comic and tragic
         leading lady and character
Memorized many thousands of lines
         worked on her comic timing
         by counting the size of the laughs
         and felt the absolute silence
         of an enthralled crowd

She knew how to fall onstage
         and could glide down stairs
         as though she were floating on air

She could project her voice for an ampitheatre
         or a tiny off-off Broadway stage

Still she was an outsider at auditions
         she had no New York stories to tell

When she was asked, "Where did you study?"
         they didn't mean what college did you attend
Her dream was to work with Joseph Papp
         at Shakespeare in the Park

He had been a Communist in the thirties
         who believed theater should be free to see
         and that artists should receive a union wage

I had auditioned there for Henry IV but failed

Then one day his casting director called and said
         he needed a Lady Capulet

"Joe sees Juliet's mother as a fashionable young woman
         who is bored with her life
         dress for the audition "

I wore a brown nylon mini dress
  with long drooping sleeves
  a big violet straw hat
  a lavender umbrella
  and--oh--the shoes

Mustard yellow Italian leather slings
  with kitten heels and apple green hose
  and I sashayed in—already knowing the lines

Joe called for the Juliet to come and read with me
  and I knew the role was mine

I was taken for a night on the town by Romeo
  the young Martin Sheen—a consummate pro
  who sprang like a cat onto Juliet's tomb

I almost had an affair with the man who played Tybalt
  used that as subtext that the lady was secretly in love
  which is why she couldn't stop screaming
  when her cousin Tybalt was killed
  and had to be carried away by her lord
  the tall and strong Moses Gunn

My costumes were designed by Theoni
  the Tybalt's real world wife
  and one of them almost did me in

It was a ball gown of lavender silk
  shot through with real silver thread
  so light it floated above the ground
  But it staticked the lavalier mike that I wore
  ruining the illusion of natural sound

Joe said to cut the costume and Theoni said "No"
  I was caught in between—a problem to him

He told me to stay and make it work
  The engineer couldn't so he said
  "You have a good strong voice
  I'll turn off your mike in that gown"

So I had to match my naked voice with all of theirs
  outside in the cool damp evenings
  for 12 hours at a time

and it gave me laryngitis
with opening night three days away

Then came a coincidence
or it might have been karma

Many years before I had acted in Cleveland
at the Karamu Theater
the only Caucasian who had

One of those actors came to a dress rehearsal
and saw what trouble I was in
he was a beautiful half Jamaican—green eyed and gay

At his tiny Manhattan room he turned on the shower
and filled it with warm steam

He gently undressed me and began a massage
that must have lasted for hours

There may have been ganja in the steam
because I remember it like a dream
the next day I had my voice again

I returned the karma to him
by helping him meet Joe Papp
it was every actor's dream

Opening night went pretty well
I wasn't reviewed by the press

Who were busy attacking the never seen
pairing of a very black man (Moses)
with a very white woman (me)
to produce a Juliet with skin like cream

And, oh yes, there was no balcony
Martin stood on a ramp in the audience
to do the balcony scene

Joe was known for experiments—his Hamlet was a rave
but it didn't work for him that time
he had jumped across the color line

At the end of the run we had two parties
one for the actors--the A list
and another for the B list

which was the dancers and crew

Marty asked me to that one with him
  so we checked in at the big one
  because after all he was the star

And then I danced all night with the pros
  who waltzed me around the floor
  floating like a big feather in their arms

I did get other roles before I left the City
  not with a broken heart
  but with a new love in Santa Fe

I had Joe Papp's name to drop at auditions
  and the portrait in the violet silk gown
  like a woman in her wedding dress
  it made me ever so briefly a queen.

NEW MEXICO – A NEW-OLD WORLD

Its mountains, its food, its people
Enchantment
I began to live every day from sunrise

On Camino Militar

my joy at these mountains
mammary mountains of Santa Fe'
through my kitchen window
dos titos tip the sky
and now I see I'm standing
on a greenly bellied woman
my little house her womb

thank goddess my world has changed
from sick cement and stone
and that I have arrived
before all the gentle ones are gone

Quick Sketch

A tall tough cowboy squinting in the sun
        one blue eye habitually closed
        but watching me also with one eye
        then the invitation to coffee
        he knows I'm not from here by my eyes
He puts "cowboy coffee" on to boil
        "full of cow dung and other bad things
        have to beat it back into the cup with a spoon"
He turns to me and finds my New York theater past
        and suddenly a revelation
        in his rodeo days he'd followed a troupe
        on the road I guess he means
        from town to town
"They taught me how to live
        but it's been three years now and you lose it
        they would take a midnight swim
        and they could make you see a leaf
        like you'd never seen it before"
Appreciation of actors
        those who live in the now
        the artists of the first time
        not in Chicanos or in the hip
        but in a 45-year-old cowboy
        living on a hidden desert ranch
Frosty—a good cowboy name—
        "Are you one of them oddballs--sensitive I mean"
        "Yes" I said--"Aren't you?
        Doesn't anyone ever hurt your feelings?"
        "Nope," he says and now he's back on cue
        "Never let 'em get that close"
And he goes out to his sweating buckskin
        seventeen hands high and hard to handle
        the cows are sold—only four remain
        but he's moving with the times

He's training jockeys for the track--girl jockeys
     and he's proudly flashing back the hate he gets
     for being a bachelor there with girls
     "Them Texans is worried about their dirty little daughters"
Does he ever lose his iron control or not?
     too bad he has to need it

Snake Dance

The Hopi bring the snakes in from the desert
      Racers, rattlers, bull snakes
They go into the kiva with them for three days
      When they emerge, the dance begins

Judy and I drove there in the August heat
      With a homemade sand candle as a gift
So we could sit on someone's roof on the plaza
      Like hundreds of pilgrims from far away

The cacique' lectured us in a very loud voice
      Sounding angry that we were there
"We don't do this for you to watch—it's a sacred dance
      We've done it for thousands of years

Don't scream or run when the snakes are released
      Don't block the way when the snake priests come through
If you understand all this, you are welcome
      You can be our guests and eat with us"

The drums led two priests into the plaza
      One held the snake's head in his mouth
The other followed him with a feather
      Lightly stroking the snake over his shoulder

When he set it on the ground it slithered free
      Until he swiftly moved to pick it up
When he finally dashed for the exit
      His arms were swathed in snakes

We visitors had been holding our breaths
      Trying to be good Anglos and show respect
But when we all got up to leave together
      The roofs almost buckled under our feet

A Navajo told me once that the Hopi
      Pulled the rattlers' fangs before the dance
I don't think so—they truly know those snakes
      As truly the snakes know them—they are brothers

TEACHING IS LEARNING

The Middle East in Denver

Teaching is learning
Fascinated by their worlds
Which they brought with them

The Lost Prince

It was 1978 and I was teaching at CCD in Denver
Suddenly we were inundated with young Arabs
Saudis, Kuwaitis, Emirates
Their countries had sent them to become engineers
Twenty-one years old and they were free
No religious guard to watch what they did
They needed core courses and better English
I needed money and ESL tutees
The Saudis were really good-looking
With long lashes and black eyes and golden skin
Faculty at CCD didn't want them around
They talked in Arabic and studied in groups
And--the worst sin--debated their grades
I helped them write about the life of Mohammed
And Islamic art and socialist monarchy in Kuwait
I had a chance to teach oral theater and they filled up the room
I convinced them to wear their robes and do Bedouin songs
Sitting on a beautiful carpet to the beat of a drum
For us Americans it was a revelation
They followed me to a business communication class
In a school building in Aurora on the other side of town
And to a cross cultural course in etymology
Where they could show the history of their very long names
And of words like *al gebra* and *adobe--at tub* to them
I helped them get credits and they helped my classes to go
I let them confer on answers and bargain over grades
I knew it was their culture—they just had to try
But when I pointed my finger and said, "I gave you a B"
They threw up their hands as though in a *souk*
I had won—it was fine—they had tried

On Fridays, I met them at a belly dancing club
The dancer performed especially for them and they
Danced with her and paid her--not touching her skin
After 2:00 a.m. when it closed, we went to their condos
Where they cooked *kapsah* and put on their *thobes*
Their closets were full of the white silk robes

And they let me wear one so I could sit among them
Relaxed and cool in a circle on the floor
Eating rice and lamb with only the right hand
They sang and laughed and told me of their world
They called me Nora, which is an Arabic name
Although they were hated and envied by men
They were like a magnet to both women and girls
They loved dancing--they gave parties and gifts
Drove Firebirds and Cadillacs and other hot cars
I know it's hard to believe but they liked women
Even as they spoke of their mothers with love
It doesn't mean that women were their friends
More like precious pets to be covered in gold
And kept safe from the dangers of the world

It was on one of those nights that I met the Rashid prince
He was studying in London and visiting with them
He had a body servant who he lied was only his friend
But they did a tribal dance one night and at the end
The man threw himself at the feet of his prince
Full length on the floor with his arms outspread
And received a royal signal that he could stand
You see, when the Wahabi Sauds took power
They tried to kill all the males of the ruling Rashid clan
My students really hated to be called Saudis
"We are not of the Sauds--we are just Arabs," they said
The prince brought out a photo of a dead young man
Who'd gone to college in Denver and when he went home
Had gone to the palace and tried to stab the king
They had all seen him beheaded and they pitied him
The prince said he'd be killed if they found the photo on him
"They'll kill you too if you're here when they come"
It was silent for a while and then he spoke again
"I want to be a great writer—you're an English teacher
If I'm to become great, must I write only the truth"
I caught my breath but I had to say it, "Yes, I think you do"
He nodded, "I was afraid of that" he said
He returned to London and I never heard of him again

Nor of the beautiful young men who so wanted it to change
Who sometimes returned in the fall with new wives
So they could learn English and drop their veils and be free
But they were too few against the power of Islam and the Saudi king
They are fifty-eight now—their youth and beauty long gone
Did they turn into conservative, wealthy, old men
And, I wonder, did the lost prince write only the truth
And if he did, was he murdered in its name?

The Persians

In the late 70s when I had Arab students in Denver
I also had Iranians who were in their late 20s
They were modern-day men and thus easy to talk with
Amazing cooks who made their own fresh mint yogurt
It cured me of Montezuma's revenge when nothing else would
One of these men who came from an upper-class family
Taught me how the Zoroastrian Persian Empire
Had been conquered by Islamic Arabs who poured
Out of the Saharan desert and brought the Koran to them
"We still speak Farsi and we will always be Persians" he said
It was the time of the anti-Shah rebellion in favor of Khomeini
I walked in a street march with them and he whispered to me
"The Persians always make the same mistake
Dreaming that the next ruler will be The One
But he's always worse than the one before"
In those days the newest video camera was a Super 8
Some student had received a black and white silent film
Of a gigantic street march in Teheran against the Shah
They showed it on campus and I went with them
I was, as usual, the only one of Us in the room
They watched silently—then the marchers were fired on
One man bent near the camera and when he stood
He held up his bloody hand and a roar arose in the room
"Allah ilaha illa Allah "--at least a hundred voices as one
The hair stood up on the back of my neck
When the lights came on, they seemed normal again
I knew it was not a few dissidents as our government said
It was a massive uprising against the Shah
Before long he fled into exile where he soon died
Pictures of Khomeini now hung on the walls of everyone's room
With his white hair and beard and fierce, forbidding eyes
Their money from home couldn't get through
They had only I-20 visas that didn't allow them to work
So they were forced into bar tending and American marriage
Unless they went back to the dangerous land Iran had become

The final event I attended with them was an engagement party
Given by a woman graduate in engineering from UCD

It was for her younger sister before they went back to Iran
I sat on a couch with two white crows fully covered
Who shrank from me like the Great Satan himself
Our hostess was dressed in army fatigues with a cap on her hair
She pulled us all to our feet for dancing to Persian folk music
I saw how beautiful she was—how charismatic—glowing with life
Soon I went to the Philippines to teach in a Vietnamese refugee camp
Often in the UN office in Manila I saw Iranians camping on the floor
Begging for refugee status so they could hide on a far-distant island
And not be killed in Manila as followers of the Shah
Years later I returned to Denver and I met one of them again
He had become an airplane mechanic and he had a story to tell
"One of our engineering students went back and was killed"
A vision of her face appeared in my mind
He didn't even say her name, but I knew
She had started a little printing press with two male friends
Just as she had in Denver to print the underground news
And they had all been hanged as enemies of Allah
They had even killed her name—they said she was a whore
"But she couldn't have been that—she was an engineer"
"She didn't have that printed on her forehead, did she?"
Those sanctimonious old men could not stand a woman
Who was beautiful and intelligent and brave and free
They had to destroy her so other women would be afraid
I don't know if she's remembered after all these years
There have been so many martyrs in the name of Islam
I do feel sorry it's been so long I can't remember her name
If only she hadn't been so naive—believing it all would change
Now that the Shah and the Savak were gone
I know there are many Persian women like her in Iran
Who marched against covering themselves in black
Who are beautiful and intelligent and brave
And I profoundly hope that their time has come to be free

REFUGEE SUITE

Teaching is loving
The purest love there is
Between student and teacher

Freedom
For a young Vietnamese man who had to make a "Sophie's Choice"

I
having love
you gave it up for freedom
and now in freedom
you have lost your love

if she stays in Viet Nam
you are lonely here
and if she risks that pirates' hell
could be consumed

I know you feel your single flame cannot illuminate the blackness of this
Colorado sky. I think your gentle breathing blame could warm the sun

II
whispering your music
not whispering her name
you're calling for your love
until she comes again

whispering your music
thinking of her pain
dreaming of your love
until she's yours again

Celebrating UN Day at the camp.

Wearing an *aó dai* made by my students.

In front of my house in the camp with baby gecko.

Outside my UN central education office. The door was UN blue.

Pulling a Vietnamese fishing boat onto the shore with the UNHCR field officer, Bob Groelsema. Photo credit: Dwight Russell

The fishing boat displayed inside the Vietnamese Refugee center on Palawan Island in the Philippines.

On Palawan Island—1984

I drove in the UNHCR vehicle on jungle roads you could barely see
Forded streams—not even knowing where they were going
I walked by night among cobras and by day among scorpions

and I wasn't afraid

On New Year's Eve I put on my UN T-shirt and marched to the guard
house Where drunk Filipinos were shooting M-16s--Vietnamese children
all around. I told them it was dangerous--to put the rifles away and they
did

and I wasn't afraid

At the Bataan Processing Center I gave a note to the UN man from
Geneva Right in front of his military escort in order to tell him of their
abuses. I was arrested and taken to the refugee jail until the UN got me
out

but I wasn't afraid

When a Filipino soldier came to my little house in the middle of the night
I wrapped a sheet around me, turned on the light and ordered him out
In my best theater voice—pointing at the door like a queen and he went

I wasn't afraid

True, I did have the UN at my back but so did the other women UNV
And they were afraid of everything and couldn't wait to leave Palawan
But I was on a mission in that Vietnamese Refugee Center   .

and I had no need to be afraid

I was an English teacher and I lived in a kind of radiant joy
On the night of my goodbye party, Chau, my love, made a button
"Teaching is loving" it said—he drew little pink flowers on it for me

he knew I wasn't afraid

26

Back in America I dreamed of standing on a beach
Looking at a great golden Sphinx—she looked back at me
Then she slowly turned away—my radiant life was gone

and once again I was afraid

On Leaving the Philippines
March 2, 1984

you who swam near the wild monkeys' home
you whose sleeping face was like a sensual god's
whose arm was my night-long pillow
and whose burning eyes were like a judge
such a soccer-playing, palm-tree climbing boy
such a hardworking, eloquent and courteous man
a man's man, a woman's man, a refugee
the day you lost your number, Chau, were lost to me
now I who came flying back for you
am tired—am finished—and must return
who fear loneliness must board the plane alone
and you whom I approach in space
recede as I draw near
the thread so thin connecting us
falls into the ocean here

WOMBATS AND COBRAS

Australia and Cheung Chau
Two unique islands
Infuriating but funny

Wombat

A Yank in Aussieland – 1984

Is it a small pig or a big rat?
It's neither—it's a wombat!
Tasmania offers cuddling with a baby one as a prize
It made me remember a wombat story of mine own
I was in Sydney when I first saw one
Now koalas are sleepy charmers
And red kangaroos are kings
But a wombat will make you laugh in surprise
So when I made a collect call to my bank in the U.S.
Having run out of money in the first two weeks
The Aussie operator asked me
"What's your favorite thing about Oz?"
I, of course, said "the wombats"
"It's such a shame about them," quoth he
"Why, what's wrong with them?"
"There's been a massacre"
"Oh, no, it can't be true"
"They found them lying on their backs
With their feet in the air"
And then the call went through
I told some Aussies in a hushed, shocked tone
And they almost collapsed they were laughing so hard
"They're not dead—they sleep with their feet in the air"

And that was how I learned what it means to be a Yank in Aussieland

I compounded my sin at a pub
By asking for a Foster's Ale
"And make it cold, please"
"'ow do you think we serve them," the waitress growled
"Well I know the English drink warm beer"
"We ain't pommies then, are we?"
I looked it up in a book called "Speakin' 'Strine"
I had only done the "As" and hadn't gotten to "beer"
Sure enough it said, "Always served cold
And be careful, it's stronger than you think"

I visited with a Vietnamese family I knew from Palawan
They had been refugees who were resettled in Sydney
And they were sewing at home from morning to night
While they were out, a worker came to the door
"Oi 'ave somethin' 'ere for Nguyen" he grunted
And I had no idea what he said
I saw it was a sewing machine and let him in

'Strine' is indeed a different language from ours
I studied my little book and passed my "exam"
On the bus to Melbourne by laughing at
The nonstop joking stories that the driver told
We stopped for lunch by the side of the road
Ate chicken at a table with a red-checked cloth
I had a chance to stay with an Aussie family there
And all thirteen of them came to dinner
To watch the Yank eating vegemite on toast
And trying to pretend she liked it
I asked them to teach me some rhyming slang
One of them slapped his thigh and said,
"The septic tank wants to learn our rhymes"
"Tank" rhymes with "Yank" and there I was
If you don't laugh, they'll never stop teasing
But if you can take it--they'll let you in

I loved the lifestyle—they worked hard in the morning
Drank Foster's at lunch and slacked off in the afternoon
I wanted to move to Adelaide in South Australia
Because it was old-fashioned and friendly
And had a lovely theater—a mini Sydney opera house
Where I saw a play about fighting the fires
That rage in from the Outback
How everyone drops whatever they're doing
And rushes outside the cities to fight them
I bought small pieces of aboriginal art
A wooden lizard and a landscape burned on bark

Back in Sydney a group of people I'd known in the camp
Offered to pay me to teach them English if I would stay
But I had a two-month visa that an Embassy man

I knew in the refugee camp had gotten for me
He'd pushed it through in Manila almost overnight
And he'd made me promise not to overstay
I said a tearful goodbye to my "daughter" Thuy Hang
At the airport, believing I would return before long
I ended up in Hong Kong at another refugee camp
And then became a *gaijin* in Japan
So I never made it back to Aussieland
To hug the wombats and feed apples to the wallabies
See the fairy penguins swimming to shore at twilight
Smell the eucalyptus air
Hear the "kookaberra laughing in the old gum tree"
And be a Yank again

Cheung Chau Island waterfront

On Cheung Chau Island - 1993

Cheung Chau is a bedroom suburb for Hong Kong
Its charming waterfront restaurants
Let you choose your fish while it's swimming around
For half the price you'd pay on the mainland
I met an American expat there
Who needed someone to pet sit her rabbit
While she spent a few weeks in Bangkok
Of course, I told her "Yes"
My name was adventure then
She only warned me about one thing
It took a boat ride from Cheung Chau to
Where her apartment was in Newtown
And it should cost one Hong Kong dollar
"Don't pay any more or you'll ruin it for me"
They'll try to charge you the *gwailo* price"
Gwailo—ghost--I'd never met real prejudice before
I might have been *gaijin*—outsider--in Japan
But there everyone paid the same
How could such a small thing ruin it all
But I dreaded the struggle every day
Once the boatman screamed in Chinese at me
While I clutched the wooden bench
And the commuters yelled at him to let it go
I had to cross for shopping and for the pubs
Nothing else to do and the apartment was cold
I learned that there was an overland route
Through the graveyard of steles facing the sea
One dark evening I rambled through it
To the other side and to the British pub
Naturally, I mentioned that I'd walked from Newtown
"Oh, my dear," the English lady looked horrified
"Don't you know that there are cobras there"
"I know, I stamped on the ground to scare them away"
"My dear--they drop from the trees"
"Oh," I said
"When my husband and I first moved here years ago

I opened a cupboard and stuck my hand in and a cobra bit me
My husband cut above the bite and sucked the poison out
And spat it on the floor and rushed me to Hong Kong
My arm swelled and hurt a bit but I lived
When we came back to the house
There were green crystals on the floor
Now when I open a cupboard, I look inside
If one is in it, I wave my arms and say 'Shoo, cobra'"
I took a boat that night and never walked overland again

MY JAPAN

The Japan I found
Belongs to me alone
The lessons I learned
Are everyone's

at the Hasadera
only *ema* bloomed
thank you Kannon
for this rose

brief as cherry blossoms in the spring
a young man's love
for the towering tree on which he leans

Note: ema are small wooden boards on which prayers are written, to be burned later to send the messages to the goddess of mercy

Dr. Chiaki Mukai—My Japan

When I first met her where she worked in a room full of people,
The humble woman could have been an Office Lady
Delivering tea--and not what she really was—an astronaut.
My Tokyo school asked me to teach her wherever she could.
They paid me 30,000 yen for a 3-hour class--$300--
But you learn to think in yen and not as one American,
Have your daughter mail tooth paste from the US,
Because it was $15, but really it was only1500 *yen.*
iSS taught simultaneous translators how to be so good
That they would be hired by NHK and the UN.
It was very near the Emperor's palace grounds--
I went to watch the gardeners training the young trees;
They staked their limbs to the ground like giant *bonsai*--
Royal trees couldn't grow just however they chose.
I watched one class where they shadowed CBS news;
I recorded many articles about science and business,
For they needed fresh material to translate every week.
I read in short phrases   with long pauses   for beginners;
Then longer phrases and shorter pauses   for intermediates;
And finally as fast as we normally speak without pauses.

Dr. Mukai spoke English fluently but she needed special help--
She would be interviewed as Japan's first woman astronaut,
And she would have to answer quickly and well.
I liked her —she was so friendly and down to earth,
But she would have left it forever if she could.
She was married and a heart surgeon, but she longed for space.
"Would you go to a space station, if you could never come back?"
She said "yes" in a heartbeat.
"Was it difficult for you as a woman to become an astronaut?"
"No."--I knew that would never fly with the Western press.
"Chiaki-san, were you the only female in medical school?"
"Yes."
"And didn't you have to be twice as good to succeed?"

"Yes."
I taught her to say "yes" and "no"—"yes" as a student, but not now.

When I wasn't tutoring her, I had an intermediate class
Who were paying—not an arm and a leg, but a silk kimono--
A custom-made pure silk kimono and embroidered *obi*--
That is 1 to 3 million yen--to go to this famous school.
One class had American newspaper articles as lessons.
Imagine standing in front of a group of 25 young people,
All of whom have a fantasy of America and want to travel here,
None of whom do Halloween or understand witches or Satan,
And telling them that on a certain night of the year, Americans
Keep their black cats inside, or they might be killed by Satanists.
Clearly, I didn't choose that article. A Japanese administrator,
Who wrote glossaries from his bilingual dictionary, had done so;
I saw that they had mistakes in idioms and tone.
I didn't want to mislead the students, so I approached him
With lots of *"Sumimasen"* and *"Arigato gozaimasu,"*
Bowing with arms folded so that he wouldn't be offended,
And he started showing them to me before printing them.
The school decided to let the *gaijin* teachers
Offer one class of our own choosing each term.
My first choice was American Comedy Videos--
"Three's Company" and "All in the Family" were on TV.
I transcribed entire scripts from the videos for them.
First showing, they laughed a little and we talked about it;
I handed out my glossary of odd American customs;
The second showing, they laughed more,
And I answered questions for as long as they wanted;
The third time, they laughed all the way through,
And it was satisfying both for them and for me.
Another time, I taught American Poetry,
Using "John Brown's Body" by Stephen Vincent Benet.
These women knew all about our Civil War--
What they didn't know was that Americans have poetry.
English for them was technology and business and news.
I'd performed this narrative epic in college,
So I made tapes for them to shadow at home.
When we read in class, they all sounded like me,

But it had rhythm and a sort of Southern accent—
It was very satisfying for them and for me.
My most popular class was Speed Reading.
It drew 50 people—more than any other class.

Here's how you do it—let them choose a novel;
Make a cardboard reader with holes for half lines;
Time them reading for five minutes through the holes;
They can't go back and they have to read faster than usual.
Then, you have them free write all they can remember;
Take up the books, and next class do it again and again.
To their surprise, the faster they read, the more they remember.
We know that it's because English is so redundant--
You don't need every word if you stop sub-vocalizing.
They became able to enjoy reading novels in English--
And it was very satisfying for them and for me.

Outside of Dr. Mukai's office, I saw a model of a spaceship
To be made by both Japanese and Americans.
It was silver and elegant—beautiful and inspiring,
But it never happened because NASA lost its funding.
One of the last things she asked me in a wistful tone,
"Eleanor *sensei,* why don't people think space is important?"
"You're standing on an iceberg, *Chiaki-san*, and looking at the sky;
They are under water and they can't see what you see."
I got a postcard from her at the aerospace station in Texas,
When I had returned and was living in Denver.
I had a handshake agreement that I could teach at iSS again,
And I flew back to Tokyo months later on that handshake--
I knew they would not dishonor their word.
However, I didn't have a place to live and I could not rent one.
Landlords did not trust *gaijin* and were quite free to refuse us.
I had to tell my class that I couldn't finish the term,
Because I was living in a hostel and paying by the night.
A young woman named Momoko offered to let me live with her,
And that began a new chapter of my life inside Japan.

I'd like to describe her at 25 when she was wild and wore jeans;
And how at 26 she was "Christmas cake" till she married quickly.
How a little baby sleeps on its back on a futon with its mother;
Tell who gives chocolates on Valentine's Day and who on White Day;
How a radio program told the whole country what to say,
If asked why Japan wasn't sending troops to fight in Kuwait;
About Emperor Hirohito's death after a long illness;

How they canceled Xmas because of it and didn't use the color red
Or give year-end parties, in respect for their father the Emperor;
How an elegant lady named Ishii studied poetry with me,
Showed me her *hana matsuri* dolls from 1942,
When she had fled Tokyo to escape our bombing,
And how she taught me the art of *ikebana;*
How I got a Canadian soccer player fired from iSS,
Because he seduced my 19-year-old virgin student and
When she went to see him, closed the door in her face.
She cried to me that he had used her like a yellow taxi;
How an enormous *sumo* fighter walked in Tokyo like a *samurai;*
How my modern girls dressed in kimono on Coming of Age day
And turned into beautiful *geisha* fantasies of themselves,
Clattering pigeon-toed in their *geta* on the cobblestones,
As they went to a Shinto temple to celebrate being 20 years old.
These are some of my treasured stories of life in Japan.
You may know someone who lived there, but tells another story,
For every *gaijin* who lives there, discovers a different Japan.

Dr. Chiaki Mukai and her English tutor

STEWART 先生 ㊞

I.S.S. INTERPRETER TRAINING CENTER

Sogo Kojimachi Dai-2 Bldg. 5I
1-6 Koji-machi, Chiyoda-ku, Tokyo 102, Japan
Tel:(03)265-7103 Fax:(03)265-7110

特別クラス

```
 O r a l   R e a d i n g   o f   A m e r i c a n   L i t e r a t u r e

Some of you many recall the last time ISS offered this service class.  Eleanor
Stewart has returned from the U.S and will teach another American dramatic
narrative poem, entitled "John Brown's Body" by Stephen Vincent Benet.  The
poem centers around the Civil War period from 1861 - 1865.  She directed and
performed in this readers' theater adaptation while in the U.S. and has
prepared a casette tape for use in the class.  Her teaching method utilizes
the shodowing technique for improvement in intonation, rhythm and emotional
coloring in the use of English.

Instructor: Eleanor Stewart
```

日　時：1月16日・23日・30日・2月6日・13日（水）合計5回
　　　　午後3時～5時

受講料：20,000円

申込方法：下記の受講申込書の必要事項をご記入の上、1月16日に受講料を添えて
　　　　お申し込み下さい。（締切日：1月11日）

アイ・エス・エス通訳研修センター

千代田区麹町1-6 相互麹町第2ビル5F

☎ 03-265-7103

- - - - - キ リ ト リ - - - - -

受講申込書

氏名＿＿＿＿＿＿＿＿＿＿

[氏名英文：　　　　　　　　]

[番　　]

電話　（　　　）

領収証

　　　　　　　　　　　様

受講費用として20,000円
を領収いたしました。

平成3年　　月　　日

アイ・エス・エス通訳研修センター

千代田区麹町1-6 相互麹町第2ビル5F

A free elective class for advanced students in English

Ishii-san, who had lovely English and who knew a lot
about our Civil War from her studies at a Catholic college.

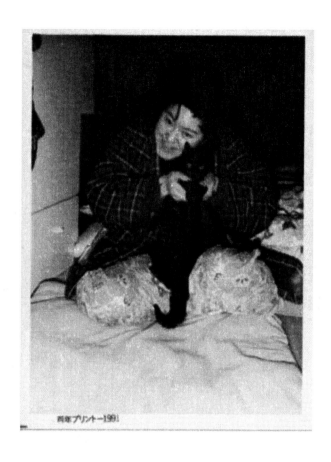

Momoko and her cat Pyong-Pyong

Dinner out with my darling girl students who loved being with their *sensei*. Much giggling.

Their transformation into classic beauties on Coming of Age Day in January, when everyone celebrated turning 20 on the same day.

Reverse Culture Shock

"Did you learn Japanese?"--they always ask me that
"Do you speak Japanese?"--they request to be impressed
And when I answer, "Only a few words," they're not

"Wait," I try to say. "I read fifty of their novels
I studied the Tokyo train maps like a bible
And I can go anywhere now alone

I fell into enchantment there
Took great photos of temples and roofs
Of street scenes and lovely women friends

I rode a tall bike built for ladies' skirts
Ate *sushi* with Chu-hai lemon squashes
And transparent blowfish *sashimi*

Drank Pocari Sweat when I sweated
Green tea with popped rice when it was cold
Dry Asahi minis from a neighborhood machine

I loved teaching American comedy and poetry
And kept a list of fascinating nouns
Koneko and *koseki*

Omikuji and *tatsu no otoshigo*
"little dragon that fell from its father"
A perfect Nihon image of a seahorse

I lived in a brand-new little mansion
With a ladder to the clean white wooden loft
Nihon in my purse and someone to love

I could say *"Gomen asai"*
Feel comfortable in silence
And safely walk at midnight

"Wait, don't go—there's so much more"
But they're already gone
Clutching their clichés like handbags

They don't need my stories
They know everything about Japan
They read headlines and watch TV

I was culture shocked for half a year
Before I found my *gaijin* way
Reverse shock won't ever go away

O Manju

I have an addiction only I can understand
It's little soft cushions of sticky rice
With red mung beans inside
Dusted with powdered sugar and frozen
In Japan they are street food
Fresh and on a stick
In autumn at temples they are cooked in sake'
And the scent alone is like a prayer to Buddha
If we pass an Asian market I beg my friend to go in
And bring me back a six pack
I can't leave the parking lot till I've eaten four
Taste and scent—the only true memoir

CATS IN MY WORLD

Cats have been my friends
My whole life
And still are

Genki

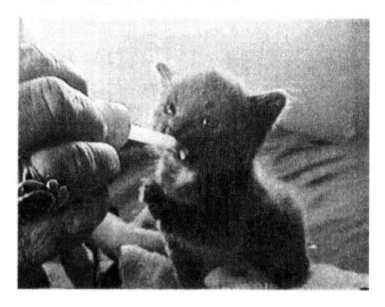

Genki

In Japan, "O genki desu ka?" means literally, "Is your vital energy strong?" The answer is, "Genki, des".

The mews were tiny but penetrating
After a couple of hours we went over the wall
To the complex next door
Three of them looked like their mother
White with yellow ears
The fourth was a gray furry ball
So we got a box and started to pick them up
A young man came out, "You'd better get them out of here
I'm letting out my German shepherd"
We went to the nearby shelter
I began handing them over
But the gray one just stuck to my hand
We named him Genki, as kittens always are
He grew into a long-legged Russian blue
So tall he could stand beside me at the sink
And I could pet him without leaning down
So tall that he swiped a hummingbird from the sky
And presented it to a horrified me
He had his own unique way of talking
He swooshed his paws up and down
On the wall, the sink, the mirror, a painting
Once our manager heard it going swoosh swoosh
And asked if there was a water leak somewhere
No, I said and opened the closet door
It was just Genki trapped inside
He didn't cry, he only swooshed
Then one night we heard him scream outside
My housemate ran out to lift him up
But he couldn't stand—his legs wouldn't work
We drove him to the vet but he stood up on the counter
And he seemed all right
He was two and a half years old
When it happened again on a Sunday
We took him to the VCA and told how he would scream
And then be paralyzed for a while

She said, "He has an enlarged heart and he's going to die
I suggest you do it today"
Now, I was the one who screamed
"No, no, what are you saying?"
"I'll give him an X ray and show you
We'll anesthetize him"
She carried him away looking back at me
With wide innocent green eyes
I drove to Urgent Care down Montgomery
I was frantic and almost babbling
Can you do an X-ray without anesthetic on a cat
"Of course," so I drove back to VCA
Rushed past the desk to the back room
Grabbed him from the cage and carried him out
Stopping only to pay $100 at the desk
Urgent Care wrapped him in a blue blanket on a little bed
And told us to come back the next day
He had cardiomyopathy—just like a human
When I saw the ultrasound of his tiny heart pumping
As he lay calmly while I stroked his head
One side was so much bigger and I sobbed silently
So we gave him pills and special food
I couldn't sleep waiting for him to scream
I would massage his hind legs
Over and over so they wouldn't atrophy
That worked for a while—until it didn't
He got better but one leg was desiccated
He was a cat and he didn't fear
He was just a happy cat
He could still stand up and swoosh
The next time it paralyzed three of his legs
I put water next to him and he tried to drink
But only one paw worked and he gave up
I saw him drop his head
I held him between my knees
And tried to drip beef broth into his mouth
He looked up at me and it was as if he said
"I know you're trying to help me—but I can't"
A little later the last one took his lungs
I watched the light fade in his green eyes

The little swoosh was gone
He was only three years old
We had spent two thousand on vets
But we didn't care—he was our only child
But you see, he wasn't *genki* after all

The Beloved Hand

She lets him rub her under the chin
    and carry her and these days
    gently rub her tummy
But the hand she pushes her face into
    when she's lonely
    in the middle of the night
Not hungry—there's always food out—lonely
    the hand she stretches her arms
    out to when I baby talk her
    "Callie are you awake?"
Is the hand of her own person
    the beloved hand
And people say cats aren't affectionate

II – EPIPHANIES

Colorblinded

There was segregation in the schools in Parkersburg, West Virginia
    when I was a child
I went to Parkersburg High and lived at one end of
    Avery Street in a big brick house
At the other end of the long street
    there was Sumner High for Negroes
I didn't think about it—I was busy
    with my acting and my life—it was normal
In my senior year the schools were integrated
    and Sumner High was shuttered
I didn't think about that either
    there was no stone throwing or overt hostility
And there were only a few of them anyway
    nothing changed that much
I went a few miles away to college
    and on summer break I came home to work
One Sunday evening at the Presbyterian Church
    I gave a speech to the youth group
Afterward a young man of sixteen came up to tell me
    that he had seen me perform
In "The Curious Savage" my senior year
    I had dyed my hair blue with shoe polish
He wanted to be in the theater too
    and wondered if we could talk about it
So we walked back to the big brick house
    sat in the living room and talked for hours
He was black—light brown really
    and he said that there was one thing stopping him
"My skin is brown and there's nothing I can do about it.
    it will always be that way"
Epiphany! A light bulb came on.
    he might be talented and was good looking
But he was a Negro forever
    his desperation stunned me with that knowledge

A few years later I lived in Cleveland, Ohio
    I still loved acting and I had a choice
The white theater downtown or Karamu closer to home

I chose Karamu—I was colorblind
This was before black power and the civil rights movement
    and Martin Luther King
I don't remember whether the audiences were mixed
    but I was the only white actress
They took me in and taught my ignorant white self
    about things like soul food and jazz
I learned how black skin needed to be oiled or it would turn gray
    and about "do rags"
My leading man took me to a jazz club where we drank
    spiked coffee from a thermos
And heard John Coltrane and Max Roach
    the most amazing drummer I had ever seen
I was one of them—I was friends
    with the young woman tech director
She had won the respect of a local gang
    who guarded Karamu all night long
But sometimes she seemed angry with me
    for no reason that I could understand
Finally, she said, "Some days I hate all white people
    it isn't you—I just can't help it."
Epiphany! Another light came on
    they were black and they could never forget it.
I was not one of them and I never would be
    I felt the first sting of racism

You know the story of how in New York I acted
    in Shakespeare in the Park
And how a young man from my Karamu days
    saved my voice for opening night
And how Joseph Papp was blasted by the critics
    for interracial casting
Things were changing rapidly and black people
    were silent no more
That same leading man wore an afro
    and was down with Black Power
When I rushed up to hug him
    after I saw him in a Broadway show
He pulled back and looked around
    to see if anyone he knew was watching

I still thought I was colorblind
    until one day many years later in Denver
A jazzman who was called "The Hawk"
    tall, wearing a black cape, gave me the third epiphany
He said that when he walked out with a white girl
    she was busy talking and looking up at him
But he was always watching the street
    who was looking at them together and
What was the expression on their face
    it was his job to always be aware and ready
To deal with the hatred if it came
    He had always looked so cool and above it all

I knew then that I had only been colorblinded
    by my own belief that I understood
I didn't –I couldn't and I never would
    I can only keep checking myself
And being aware of those moments
    when a newspaper story or a television host
Causes me to say
    "Of course, it's because they are black"
Racism can go into remission
    but it's never really cured
So, forgive us, the colorblinded
    for our unwitting sins
Like Whoopi on "The View"
    keep teaching us with humor
Help us to see clearly
    not to give in to fear and turn away
Now more than ever we must see truly
    or we will be in civil war one day

"I Didn't Know There Was a Place Like This"

It's just Winnings _
The coffee house and study hall
Near Central and UNM
They came in off the street and sat together
Two Indians approaching middle age
A man and woman together at a table
I wheeled up to the front and asked her
"What tribe are you?" "Navajo", she said
"And him?" I pointed to the dark man beside her
She nodded, so I opened the page that says "The Din'e"
In my published book of poetry
I read the one called "Harry"
I don't know if they understood
Then I announced "Gallup Ceremonial, 1971"
And they both threw their hands in the air
Murmured together and listened closely
It's an angry poem that says
"They who are the cause now blame what they have made
When they say you need their pawnshops and their bars"
He nodded as I stopped by on the way back
And then he borrowed a guitar and got up to sing
"This will be different from anything you've heard"
He used the falsetto voice that goes so well with drums
But before he began, he said, "I love this woman so much
Her name is Melinda and I love her so much"
The song was to her and part of it was in his language
I heard a line that said, "You put on your beads for me"
I know just enough of their culture to understand
The turquoise and silver squash blossom necklace
Is only to be worn for a special man
When he sat down, she played with his necklace
A white cross--as though we weren't there
Then it was over and he came back to me
Said that the Ceremonial is worse than ever
And told me they had no place to stay
They're from Gallup and know no one here
I had to say that I couldn't help, which was true
"I didn't know there was a place like this"

After he left, I tried to hide it when I cried for
That combination of innocence and alcohol
Of being gifted and too poor even to get home
It's infuriating and painful and unfair
I was glad that I was there when they came
So he would sing and play his love song
How did it feel to look in from the street
And see people singing and telling stories?
Maybe it looked like a piece of home

§

Colleagues

Bill Primm and I were teachers of public speaking at UNM
He was a lawyer who wanted to teach and I was in love with teaching
Just before Christmas that year in the 70s, there was a faculty meeting
Two new assistant profs had come from Princeton to take charge
They promised us no multiple-choice exams on the textbook
Rumors had been going around on the need for a big, bad final
He and I believed in the instructor's right to decide the grade
Public speaking is just that—learning to speak before an audience
One prof said he would sell a multiple-choice exam to the students
Rather than allow the grade to depend on it and we cheered
But the first thing we learned in January was that there was a new exam
It would count 40% of the final grade and it had been written by them
Apparently while the rest of us were on winter break
Bill and I read it together and saw that it had many mistakes
Hastily written, it had questions with two right answers
We asked graduate students to take it and sure enough
They missed a lot on a freshman test they should have aced
We told our students to hold a blank paper while they took it
And write alternate answers on questions that confused them
We graphed the results and took them to a faculty meeting
To prove that a quarter of the test needed to be thrown out
Bill and I agreed that he should present while I listened
I had an inkling of what was coming and I wasn't naive
The hotshot professors were furious and went on the attack
And here was the gist of what they said in response
They would consider throwing out some questions
 But only because of Bill's work—they would only mention him
I was too emotional they said
Even though he had yelled in the meeting
While I sat there and said not a word
Bill couldn't believe what he'd heard
He told them that we had worked together
They must credit us both or he would publish the results
''Eleanor, that's the first time I understood sexism''
The whole experience made him leave teaching in disgust
I already understood sexism—what woman my age doesn't
So, last November, the underlying bile of the Hillary haters

Showed that it wasn't about her competence or honesty
It was furious, ignorant, obvious, ugly sexism
I know there are Bill Primms out there supporting us
More now than in the 70s but never enough
We need you now—and we will never forget your name

After the Crusades

Imagine you are a young Lebanese woman
With light brown hair and big blue eyes
A Saudi man has married you and brought you to America
He's going to school while you stay home
You're pregnant and he doesn't allow you to be seen outside
Your doctor has told him you must get exercise
So he walks with you at night around the apartment complex
He brings over an English teacher to tutor him
And when he's through she works with you
You can hear him on the phone with another woman
And your blue eyes flood with tears
You don't know he's already asked the teacher
To help him find an American wife
And been told that's bigamy and it's illegal here
When your birth time comes, there's no mother or sisters
To guide you through it—only strangers in a strange room
You give him a baby girl and he blames you and walks away
He sends you off to Saudi Arabia—an unloved wife—a failure
Can you find any joy in life there
Well, your sweet baby and his mother and sisters
They will comfort you
They, too, are Arab Muslim women and they will understand

§

Hong Kong Hell – 1991

We were allowed to take the kids out of the camp for the first time
To go to a temple and see a big Buddha for they were Buddhists
They had never been on a train or held magazines and telephones
So the big Buddha couldn't compete for their attention
The 12 and 14-year olds had been born in Viet Nam
And they had walked on soft green grass before
But the five-year olds' feet knew only concrete
They'd been born in the infamous prison camp
That held the boat people somewhere outside Hong Kong
Chinese guards in towers above steel fences and 24-hour lights
They couldn't cook their own food or go outside the fence—ever
When I joined a walking tour for new camp workers
They called to me, "Co'—teach us. Please teach us English"
I so wanted to—that's why I was there
They were not accepted as refugees
They were to be forced back to Viet Nam
I wasn't allowed to teach them English and give them false hope
At my friend Myra's place that night, as I sat in silent shock
I recalled the little refugee camp on Palawan Island
With its white beach and English classes and Vietnamese food
Where I had lived for a year more than half a decade ago
And it seemed like Paradise
So, when some foreigners were needed to take children outside
I had rushed to volunteer to go with them to the temple
An adult for every two kids for fear they would try to escape
At a park we ate the cold picnic lunch, played frisbee for awhile
Then we stood back and watched them laughing and chattering
As they petted and petted and petted a stray brown mutt
We couldn't look at each other our eyes were so full of tears
We hadn't realized that they'd never touched a dog before
And that would be what they would remember of this day

On the way back, if some of them had tried to escape
I would have looked the other way and let them go
Could the streets of Hong Kong have hurt them more
Than the concrete hell they were forced to endure
For the sin of being refugee

On Lantau Island: Repatriation

She laid her head on my shoulder
"Take me home with you
Let me be your daughter"
She was just a country girl
With pink cheeks and innocent eyes
"I don't want to marry a Chinese
But I can't let them send me back"
She had been told she wasn't a refugee
She must agree to return to Viet Nam
Because the UN required agreement
The UK had sworn the camps would close
Before they gave Hong Kong back to China
After leasing it for ninety-nine years
So the men of the Hong Kong triads
Met the girls in a visiting room at the camp
And then announced they were engaged
Sometimes they were but more often
The men were pimps looking for pretty
Vietnamese—virgin and desperate
I couldn't adopt her—it wasn't allowed
I could barely get inside the camp
I wasn't UN anymore
I had a paper from a church
And then one from the Red Cross
I took the ferry from Cheung Chau to Lantau
And taught the Vietnamese translators
On the weekends when they were free
And then I ran out of money
And had to return to Colorado
I sent cash and a white silk scarf to her
I know she received them through a camp worker
He wrote that she was all right—not to worry
But what did he really know
She hadn't told him about her Sophie's Choice
She would risk her body and her very soul
With a strange man rather than return
Some went on hunger strikes
Some shaved their heads

Chained themselves to the steps of the plane
Rather than return to what they'd left
In Communist Viet Nam
I don't know what happened to them
I do know that I gave the ones who had English
A few hours of stories and laughter
In their new language that they loved
They didn't believe it when I described
The VRC on the island of Palawan
How people studied and cooked their own food
Were able to go into town until curfew at 10:00
Of course we had no riots in that small camp
People had hope and just enough power over their lives
But Hong Kong did have riots--and people died
Southerners turned against those from the North
Who had betrayed them by agreeing to go back
And so showing the world they weren't refugees
They burned them alive in their dorms at Whitehead
During the season of New Year's—of Tet
The Hong Kong fire department wouldn't go in
On Lantau, some men had knocked down a nun
As she entered the gate and tried to escape
From an island too far away to swim anywhere
I remember men looking at me with intense eyes
When I went in but no one made a move against me
I like to think they knew that I was a teacher and
That the secret photos I made of the rolls of barbed wire
To be used for a second fence around the first
Would show their refugee story to the world
No wonder they tried to swim away
Wouldn't you? Wouldn't I?

§

Kamakura

I found a magic city
I thought it was all mine
Old temples never bombed
A side street and a shrine

An American had saved it
From bombing in the war
Kyoto, Nara, Kamakura
Were too beautiful to burn

I'd never heard of him
Just Hiroshima's tomb
Warner is his name
His face is carved on stone

It was for me he saved
Those ancient wooden doors
The golden *ichiyo* tree
The *shinto* fox shrine too

And I gave it all to you
One winter afternoon
You'd never seen a city
That never had been bombed

We met and walked its lanes
You are a modern man
Who couldn't pass the fox
That guards the sacred tomb

It seemed to me the way we met
Our love could never end
We'd transcended time and age
You were my loved one then

But now I need it back again
My ancient magic town
You stole my *Kamakura*
And bombed the magic down

Memorial to Dr. Langdon Warner at Kamakura – he saved it from being bombed in World War II.

City of Peace

I was hired in Tokyo by a language school in Hiroshima
I didn't want to go there but it was the only full-time job
So I bought a *momiji bonsai* at the Asakusa temple
And rode the Shinkansen with it trembling in my hands
Once there I was taken to dinner and to a place to live
In a ninth floor apartment across from a mall
Where an etched metal sign announced
How far it had been from ground zero
When it had been an elementary school
I was afraid to go to Peace Park--I was an American
One early Sunday morning I found the courage
And on my bicycle on the little bridge I met
An old woman who smiled *"ohayo gozaimisu"*
So on August 6th, the day of remembrance, I went again
All the statues were brilliant with paper *tsuru*
Monks chanted outside the ruins of a building
From that day of infamy when the sun exploded
I felt so guilty—so ashamed--but then
An old man with keloid scars on his face
Offered me a cup of green tea
Respectfully in both hands with a bow
And I bowed respectfully and received it
He smiled at me and I felt forgiven—he knew
Some time later I was asked in English
What I thought of the Pacific War and the bomb
"It was a terrible thing to do" but I had to add
"Japan's military caused it to happen"
The young man who needed my answer
Nodded sadly and didn't speak—he knew
There were protesters in favor of flying the rising sun flag
And those against having a symbol of war in Peace Park
They handed out flyers on both sides
As the evening arrived after a profound day
The loveliness of thousands of lighted lanterns
Floated on a river once filled with bodies
While the ashes of 10,000 unknowns
Lay under a blanket of paper cranes
Every American who is so proud of the Enola Gay

And Los Alamos and the success of the bombs
Should be required to travel to that city
One time in their lives and be forgiven
You see they didn't choose to hate us
They want to be known as a City of Peace
And have built a mosaic tower with an *origami* crane
To stand at the harbor and speak beauty instead of pain

My Poor Little Hometown

I grew up in Parkersburg, West Virginia
No one I know ever heard of it
I never dreamed I'd see it on the cover
Of a New York Times magazine
What story could it have to tell?
It's a story that we know too well
A little backwater town
And a humongous corporation
DuPont arrived when I was still a student
It brought jobs and its own engineers
I went out with one before grad school
He was both bored and boring
Chemistry was all he knew
They say DuPont now covers more ground
Than the Pentagon many times over
And for years it's been dumping its waste
Onto 66 acres of farmland and a creek
The dairy farmer said his cows were friendly
And they came when he called
Until they went mad and attacked him
They lost their hair and then they died
The water they drank bubbled with foam
A little calf died with bright blue eyes
He cut it open and its organs were green
And the farmer went to a lawyer
The lawyer took the case
Cancer clusters—people sick with
What the workers called "the DuPont flu"
Hundreds of boxes of paper docs
Forced by law into public domain
The lawyer proved that, of course, DuPont knew
What poison it was dumping in unlined pits
In the boondocks where nobody saw
DuPont tried to blame the farmer
Said he couldn't take care of his cows
But it lost in court so there will be
Reparations in the millions

Apologies and, of course, the appeal
But the people in a town of 60,000
Have already drunk their Koolaid
I left for grad school and never looked back
But, oh, my poor little hometown!

Vanilla Death

Many years ago a friend of mine
Said the White Sands look like vanilla ice cream
Such innocent fun sliding down the dunes
Ice cream cannot kill you
Your car is sitting right there
Until you cannot see it anymore
And then you are lost
The French couple were found
Separated from each other
Two little water bottles weren't enough
In the shadeless sun of July
Only the child was still alive
Yes, they took their son
Why? Why weren't they warned?
Why were they alone?
I don't believe in hovering souls
But I wish they knew their ignorance
Did not kill their child

Frozen

It was 10 degrees when they brought you in
You were limp--eyes closed
Too cold for the mercury to rise
No temperature at all
The doctors put mittens on your tiny paws
And wrapped you in a bear hug blanket
That blows warm air
And lo! you sat up
A yellow tabby kitten with gold eyes

I know one small life isn't important
Next to all the death out there
But isn't it good to know
How many people cared for you
When they could so easily have left you in the snow
Now you'll be some lonely person's joy
And she'll brag, "I have a famous cat
Who was frozen in the Colorado winter
Now she's alive and purring in my arms"

Noble Hearts

He didn't want her to go to Africa because it was dangerous
But she said, "They need help and I have to go"
Next thing she's lying in a hospital trying to breathe
And her dog has been killed by the Spanish authorities

In Nigeria the virus reached a big man's brain
And he pulled out his IVs, sprayed the room with blood
And tried to go out into the city of Lagos
The beautiful doctor and three of her nurses
Held him down and saved their city and all of them are gone

Our little young nurse was ready at 26 to lead on an ebola case
But they didn't give Nora a perfect hazmat suit
And a drop of his poison blood touched her delicate skin
She's finally recovered in an isolation ward
At least Texas showed mercy and her dog is still alive

Some would call them earth angels, some would call them fools
I call them noble hearts doing the work they trained for
And their hearts told them to do—we need them
Let's be careful with them and honor them
There aren't that many noble hearts in this ignoble world

Bentley

They took her away
She didn't even say goodbye

      Bentley--be a good dog

She's gone two lights and two darks
I'm hungry   I had to go

      I'm a bad dog

Somebody's coming in
      (bark bark)

I'm sorry   I'm really a good dog
      (Wow wow wow wow wow)

Are they taking me to her
No I'm in some room all alone

They gave me food
I miss her
I'll wait for her to come

They're taking me somewhere
I see her I see her
      (pant pant)

She said my name
      (pant pant)

I'm coming
      (bark bark)

Oh Nora I l love you
      (slurp slurp)

I'm your good dog
      (slurp slurp)

These Things Happen

Inspired by a photograph on the front page of the New York Times
October 4, 2015

A nurse bends over a wounded child
    who clutches her blouse
    and looks desperately into her face
    for hope—for life

Thank you, U.S. Military
Thank you, General Campbell
    for an unmistakable, unforgivable war crime

You knew it was a hospital
    GPS coordinates
    phone calls from there
    to the US and Afghani leaders

Still it continued for another hour
    killing the bravest doctors in the world
If they didn't die they had to watch their patients
    burn alive in the ICU

If that isn't a war crime, I don't know what is
    "Sorry" we said, "It's not unusual—these things happen"

BASTA!

"I weep for your country that I love so much"

For Francois—June, 2017

He's in his mid-twenties
And a university student
Whose fingers fly on a metal guitar
As he plays many styles of our music
    from flamenco to country
Everyone knows that France has tons of culture
    but he prefers ours
So why is he weeping
Since Trump—even foreign students have been afraid to go home
Since Trump—xenophobia is on the rise
Since Trump—America has turned away from the Paris Accords
Since Trump—intelligence has given way to idiocy
Since Trump—the Lady France gave us
    is turning her face away from refugees
Turning toward fascism
Turning toward fear and racism and greed
Away from our national parks
    and the animals who live there
Away from clean energy and the future
    away from the world
I wrote back to Francois
"I weep that you love my country so much
    I will welcome your return"

The Darkness

The metaphor: the sun disappearing and briefly dropping darkness on us--its return a sure relief

I thought it was over just like many of us naïve white liberals
Civil rights had been fought for and won in the 60s
And that was the period marking the end of racism
I was wrong and the saddest thing to realize is that
Obama as president incubated it in the darkness
Underneath the shine of his and Michele's gracious elegance
Not because of what they did, but just who they were
I liked watching his lanky, loose-limbed walk to the mike
But how the whitest males must have hated it
Not least because they can't walk that way
Their hip bones don't connect to the thigh bones like his
Nor do they have the confidence inherent in that walk
It's the confidence of a cheetah—unconscious and sure
When he knelt to let the little black boy touch his hair
When he cried for the dead children and called for gun control
And softly began to sing "Amazing Grace" at a funeral
And when he dropped the mike and brushed his shoulder
He showed us for the last time how black he is
He had been very low key about it—raceless almost
But with a sense of humor, a comic's timing and rhythm
I always wondered why white people didn't claim him too
He's half white--raised by grandparents in a white family
But the old rule still holds even though we no longer
Say "mulatto" or "quadroon" or "high yellow"
The rule is one drop of black blood makes you black
Could it be any clearer—pure racism
In the sense of unadulterated—unchanged

And now the dark shadow is spreading again
Will it be as irresistible as the eclipse
And how long will our two minutes last

Brave Hearts and Gentle People

People get old
People get weak
People can't walk any more
Just when we've refined our skills
Opened our hearts and have stories to tell
Just when we're stuffed to the gills
With music and words
The world doesn't watch us any more
We aren't the king of hearts—the queen of the May
They have places to go, things to do, people to see
And we are left like beautiful fish drowning in air
Like fading rainbows
Like vintage denim falling apart
Our brave hearts beating ever more weakly
As the natural laughter of youth
The thrown back head
The casual lifting of our weight
The sexual thrusting
Quite simply disappear
We have been gentled by pain and loss and sorrow
For ourselves and for the world
But as Dylan Thomas said,
We "do not go gentle into that good night"
We hold out our songs and words
And with them
We "rage against the dying of the light"
As Shakespeare said 400 years ago
We have "immortal longings"

The Walls of Time

The walls of time are unclimbable
They are opaque as dirt and crumbly
They shift each time you touch them
And close again as you peer through
Only the markers you left as you built
Can be found and swept of mystery
Each of us lives ahead of our history
But a memory wall can sometimes fall
And a person from one's distant past
Walks through as if it were not there
A Vietnamese man from the 80s
In the refugee camp on Palawan
Flew through time to visit me here
He left a gift that sees through walls
The computer I'm using – and this
"You didn't only teach us English
You showed us how to live again"
I have done one great thing in my life
I thought it lost behind a wall of time
But Than Trong Ai broke through
And though the wall has risen again
And though my eyes are full of tears
He gave me the courage to write on
In these my few and final years

§

Other Books by Eleanor Grogg Stewart:

FALLING INTO ENCHANTMENT: Poems from the 1970s in Santa Fe, New Mexico (Sunstone Press), 2014

NOT ONLY A REFUGEE: An American UN Volunteer in the Philippines (RoseDog Books), 2011

To order books, please email Eleanor at eleanorgrogg@hotmail.com and put the title of the book in the subject line.

About the Press

Jules' Poetry Playhouse Publications is a division of Jules' Poetry Playhouse, LLC, founded by Jules Nyquist in 2012 in Albuquerque, New Mexico. My publishing mission grew out of requests to record collaborations in poetry and art in book form so that we may realize our common bonds and to provide community support as readers and writers. www.julesnyquist.com